# A Pirate Alphabet

## The ABCs of Piracy!

by Anna Butzer

illustrated by Chris Jevons

raintree

a Capstone company — publishers for children

# A is for adventure.

Sailing the high seas, visiting secret islands and finding buried treasure – pirates had their fair share of adventure!

# is for bounty.

A bounty was a reward given for the capture of a pirate. In the eyes of pirates, a high bounty was a sign of strength. It meant that people saw them as a threat.

BOUNTY

Captain Messy Beard

£2.99 Reward!

 # is for **captain**.

Pirate captains did not wear flashy clothes. Captains were captured first! To avoid being captured, captains dressed like the rest of the crew.

# D is for Davy Jones's Locker.

Way down deep, as deep as can be, is Davy Jones's Locker – the bottom of the sea. Davy Jones was the evil spirit of the sea. "Going to Davy Jones's Locker" meant someone had died or a ship had sunk.

 **is for eyepatch.**

Some pirates wore eyepatches to keep one eye used to seeing in the dark. Below deck, they could flip up the patch and see right away.

# F is for fight.

Pirates' lives were full of danger. Pirates always had to be ready for a fight. They battled people on the ships they attacked. Many pirates used short swords called cutlasses.

 **is for gangway.**

The gangway is a passage along either side of a ship's upper deck. Pirates also yelled, "Gangway!" to get through a crowd.

# is for hook.

A hook could be used in place of a hand. Captain Hook was even named after his hook in the book *Peter Pan*!

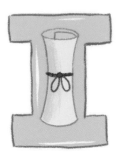

# is for island.

When they weren't sailing the high seas, pirates dropped anchor on uncharted islands. Pirates might have used islands as a place to hide from the law.

# J is for Jolly Roger.

The most famous pirate flag was the Jolly Roger. When sailors saw the skull and crossbones, it always meant one thing ... pirates!

 # is for knots.

When it comes to sailing, knots are almost as important as the wind. A poorly tied knot could threaten the safety of everyone aboard the ship.

# L is for "Land ho!"

A lookout way up in the crow's nest watched for the next place to stop. If she spotted land, she yelled, "Land ho!"

Land ho!

# M is for marooned.

Members of the crew might be marooned as punishment if they broke a rule. They would be put ashore on an island and abandoned.

 **is for navigate.**

Pirates had special tools to navigate the open oceans. They used maps, charts and compasses to know where they were.

# is for ocean.

Pirates have probably sailed the oceans as long as people have been sailing. Most people think of pirates during the 1600s and 1700s. Attacks were common in the Caribbean Sea and Pacific, Indian and Atlantic Oceans.

# P is for plunder.

No gold is safe if sea thieves are near. Hide the doubloons, silver and gold! If pirates found treasure, it was plundered and sold.

SWAG

SWAG

# is for quartermaster.

The quartermaster was second in command on a pirate ship. He made sure the crew followed the captain's orders. The quartermaster was loyal and brave.

# R is for rules.

Pirates were ruthless lawbreakers. They needed rules to help them get along. To be a part of the crew, a pirate had to agree to follow the rules.

Rules!
1. Talk like a pirate
2. Act like a pirate
3. Scrub the deck like a pirate!
4. Scrub the deck harder!
5. Eat yer greens!
6. Only parrots as pets!
7. Lights out after dinner!
8. No landlubbers!
9. Clear the deck!
10. Listen to yer Captain!
11. Plunder ye Treasure!

# is for sails.

Speed was important for pirate ships. Big ships with large sails were faster than little ships with smaller sails.

## T is for treasure.

Most people think pirate treasure was always gold and jewels. But many other items were valuable to pirates. They stole ropes, sails and tools.

# U is for underwater.

Going underwater meant a bad day for pirates. Today, people dive to see sunken ships and treasure from the time of pirates.

 **is for vessel.**

A pirate's vessel was a wooden ship. Pirates worked hard to keep their ship strong, safe and speedy. Their ship was their home.

# W is for whistle.

Pirates believed that whistling on a ship would bring stormy weather. Have you ever heard the phrase "to whistle up a storm"?

# X is for ✖ marks the spot.

Maps with an X to mark the spot probably didn't exist. Pirates would memorize where they hid their treasure and told only those they could trust.

# Y is for "Yo ho ho!"

Pirates sang songs as they worked on their ship. These songs told tales about life as a pirate. Some of these sea songs included the words, "Yo ho ho!"

 **is for zephyr.**

With a strong western wind, a ship will set sail. Across kilometres of ocean, a boat will be carried by a light breeze called a zephyr.

# Glossary

**abandoned** deserted or neglected

**compass** instrument people use to find the direction in which they are travelling; a compass has a needle that points north

**crew** team of people who work together

**cutlass** short sword with a curved blade

**doubloon** old gold coin of Spain and Spanish America

**gloom** dark or shadowy place

**phrase** group of words that expresses a thought but is not a complete sentence

**ruthless** cruel and unconcerned about others

**tale** exciting or dramatic story

**threat** someone or something that could cause harm or trouble

**uncharted** unknown territory; not on a map

# Read More

*Famous Pirates* (Pirates Ahoy!), Rosalyn Tucker (Raintree, 2015)

*Goodnight Pirate*, Michelle Robinson (Puffin, 2014)

*Pirates Handbook* (Usborne Handbooks), Sam Taplin (Usborne, 2009)

# Websites

**www.nationalgeographic.com/pirates/ bbeard.html**
Read about famous pirates.

**www.rmg.co.uk/discover/explore/ golden-age-piracy**
Find out about pirates and how they lived.

# Index

Raintree is an imprint of Capstone Global Library Limited, a company incorporated in England and Wales having its registered office at 264 Banbury Road, Oxford, OX2 7DY – Registered company number: 6695582

**www.raintree.co.uk**
myorders@raintree.co.uk

Text © Capstone Global Library Limited 2017
The moral rights of the proprietor have been asserted.

Editor: Gillia Olson
Designer: Ashlee Suker
Art Director: Nathan Gassman
Production Specialist: Katy LaVigne
The illustrations in this book were created digitally.

ISBN 978 1 4747 2444 9
20 19 18 17 16
10 9 8 7 6 5 4 3 2 1

**British Library Cataloguing in Publication Data**
A full catalogue record for this book is available from the British Library.

Every effort has been made to contact copyright holders of material reproduced in this book. Any omissions will be rectified in subsequent printings if notice is given to the publisher.

All the Internet addresses (URLs) given in this book were valid at the time of going to press. However, due to the dynamic nature of the Internet, some addresses may have changed, or sites may have changed or ceased to exist since publication. While the author and publisher regret any inconvenience this may cause readers, no responsibility for any such changes can be accepted by either the author or the publisher.

Printed and Bound in China.

# Other Titles in This Series

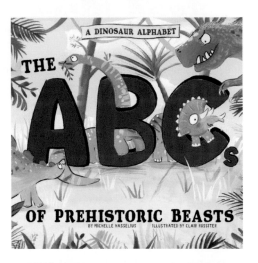